Dragonflies

ABDO
Publishing Company

Big Buddy BOOKS
Insects

Julie Murray

VISIT US AT
www.abdopublishing.com

Published by ABDO Publishing Company, 8000 West 78th Street, Edina, Minnesota 55439.

Copyright © 2011 by Abdo Consulting Group, Inc. International copyrights reserved in all countries. No part of this book may be reproduced in any form without written permission from the publisher. Big Buddy Books™ is a trademark and logo of ABDO Publishing Company.

Printed in the United States of America, North Mankato, Minnesota.
042010
092010

 PRINTED ON RECYCLED PAPER

Coordinating Series Editor: Rochelle Baltzer
Editor: Sarah Tieck
Contributing Editors: Heidi M.D. Elston, Megan M. Gunderson, BreAnn Rumsch, Marcia Zappa
Graphic Design: Maria Hosley
Cover Photograph: *Shutterstock*: Cathy Keifer.
Interior Photographs/Illustrations: *Image Ideas Inc.* (p. 9); *Peter Arnold, Inc.*: ©Biosphoto/Lefrèvre Michel (p. 25), ©Biosphoto/Henno Robert/Wildlife Pictures (p. 13), John Cancalosi (p. 30), Delpho, M. (p. 25), Fischer, B. (p. 27), Hans Pfletschinger (pp. 9, 11), WILDLIFE (p. 21); *Photo Researchers, Inc.*: Adrian Bicker (p. 17), Stephen Dalton (p. 13), E.R. Degginger (p. 9); *Shutterstock*: John David Bigl III (p. 5), BogdanBoev (p. 25), firedark (p. 23), Eric Isselée (p. 7), Kirsanov (p. 19), Dr. Morley Read (p. 15), Rose Thompson (p. 29), Fong Kam Yee (pp. 20, 30).

Library of Congress Cataloging-in-Publication Data

Murray, Julie, 1969-
  Dragonflies / Julie Murray.
    p. cm. -- (Insects)
  ISBN 978-1-61613-484-6
  1. Dragonflies--Juvenile literature. I. Title. II. Series: Murray, Julie, 1969- Insects.
  QL520.M87 2011
  595.7'33--dc22

                                    2010000788

Contents

Insect World 4

A Dragonfly's Body 6

Life Begins 8

Underwater World 12

A New Life 14

All Grown Up 18

Good Hunters 20

Fast Fliers 22

Danger Zone 24

Special Insects 28

Bug-O-Rama 30

Important Words 31

Web Sites 31

Index 32

Insect World

Millions of insects live throughout the world. They are found on the ground, in the air, and in the water. Insects have existed since before there were dinosaurs!

Dragonflies are one type of insect. They live near lakes, ponds, and streams. You may even find dragonflies in a city or in your backyard!

Bug Bite!

Dragonflies are closely related to damselflies.

A dragonfly's body may be red, green, or blue. It has white, yellow, or black markings.

A Dragonfly's Body

Like all insects, dragonflies have three main body parts. These are the head, the **thorax**, and the **abdomen**.

A dragonfly's head has a mouth, two very large eyes, and three smaller eyes. Six legs and four wings connect to the thorax. A dragonfly's abdomen is very long. Important **organs** are inside of it.

Bug Bite!

A dragonfly's large eyes take up most of its head. This allows the dragonfly to see nearly all the way around itself!

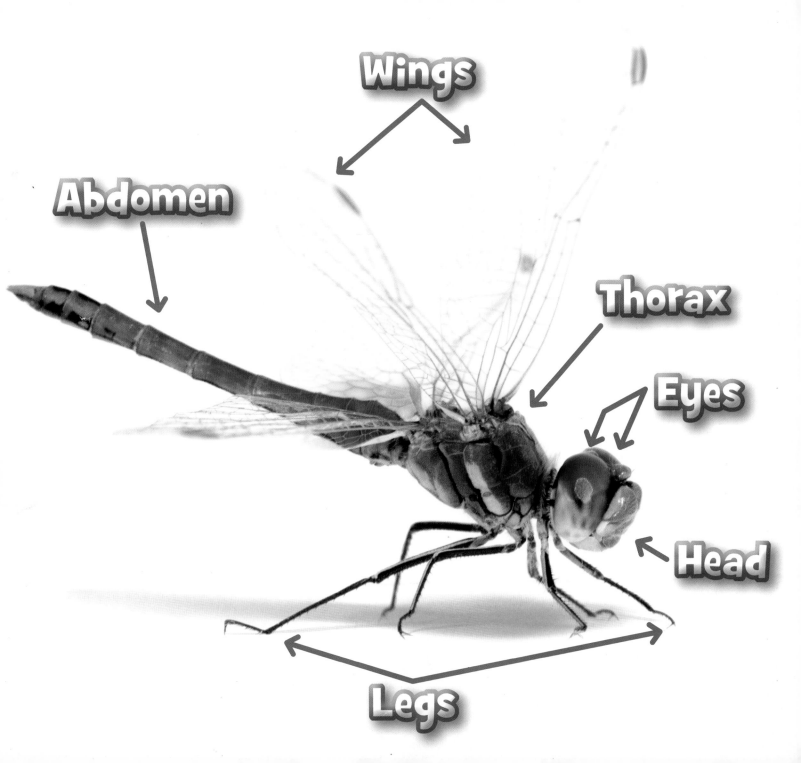

Wings

Abdomen

Thorax

Eyes

Head

Legs

Life Begins

The dragonfly life cycle has three stages. These are egg, larva, and adult. Dragonfly larvae are called nymphs (NIHMFS).

Dragonflies begin life as eggs. After **mating**, the mother dragonfly lays her eggs. The father may help her do this. Sometimes dragonflies lay eggs on plants near water. Other times, they place them underwater.

Life Cycle of a Dragonfly

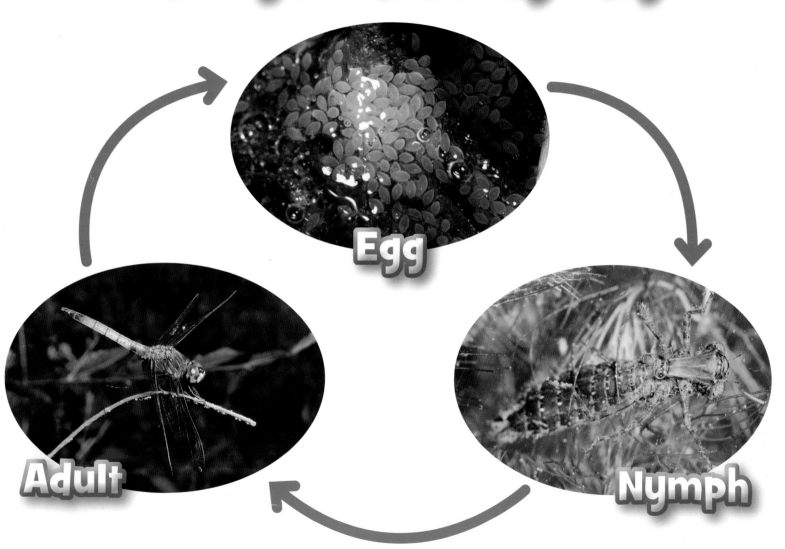

Egg

Nymph

Adult

Inside an egg, a dragonfly nymph quickly grows. It usually **hatches** within one to three weeks.

Dragonfly nymphs live in calm freshwater, such as ponds or **marshes**. There, they hunt, eat, and grow. Some nymphs spend about one year underwater. Others can live there for five years!

Nymphs have gills. This allows them to breathe underwater.

Underwater World

Dragonfly nymphs are hunters. They eat worms, tadpoles, and even small fish! Nymphs have a special mouthpart called a mask. It stretches out to catch **prey**.

As nymphs eat, their bodies grow bigger. They **shed** their skin many times. This is called molting. As nymphs molt, wings begin to form.

Bug Bite!

Sometimes, dragonfly nymphs eat other dragonfly nymphs!

A nymph's mask has hooks at the end. These help it catch and hold prey.

A New Life

When a nymph is fully grown, it crawls out of the water. Most crawl up the stem of a plant. Then, it **sheds** one last time.

Shedding skin is hard work. So, a dragonfly takes breaks to rest.

After it **sheds** a final time, the dragonfly is a full-grown adult. At first, its wings are wet and wrinkled. The dragonfly pumps blood into them. This helps harden them so it can fly.

New adult dragonflies must be careful. They are not yet strong enough to **protect** themselves by flying away. So, many predators look for them.

It can take several hours for a dragonfly's wings to dry and stretch out.

All Grown Up

Adult dragonflies live near water. They usually live from a few weeks to a year. During this time, dragonflies hunt for food. They also **mate**. They rest in hidden or safe areas.

Adult dragonflies spend much of their lives in the air. But sometimes, they rest on plants.

Good Hunters

Dragonflies are powerful predators. Their bodies are made to help them find and catch food. Their eyes allow them to see movement well. Their legs help them catch and hold on to **prey**. Sometimes, they eat their prey in midair!

A dragonfly's large eyes have many tiny lenses. These lenses work together to help the dragonfly see prey.

Dragonflies eat many kinds of insects.

Fast Fliers

A dragonfly's wings help it move quickly from place to place. Wings allow a dragonfly to move up, down, forward, backward, and sideways.

Wings also help a dragonfly hunt. They allow it to pause in midair and change direction. So, a dragonfly can easily chase and catch **prey**.

Bug Bite!

Dragonflies can fly up to about 38 miles (61 km) per hour!

A dragonfly has two sets of wings. Many are so thin you can see through them.

Danger Zone

During every stage of life, dragonflies face predators. These include fish, spiders, birds, turtles, and frogs. Insects hunt dragonflies, too. Sometimes, large dragonflies eat smaller ones!

Birds catch dragonflies in their strong beaks.

Raccoons often live near water. Sometimes they snack on dragonflies.

Bug Bite!

When dinosaurs lived, dragonflies were much larger than they are today. Some were 28 inches (71 cm) from wingtip to wingtip!

Dragonflies use their powerful bodies to **protect** themselves. They can fly away fast to escape predators. If caught, they can bite to fight back.

Dragonflies are such good fliers that they can escape most predators. But, when they can't fly away, they hide.

Special Insects

Dragonflies do important work in the natural world. They eat insect pests, such as mosquitoes and gnats (NATS). By doing this, they help control insect populations. This keeps nature in balance and **protects** life on Earth.

Dragonflies eat moths. This helps keep moths from harming plants.

Bug-O-Rama

How big are dragonflies?

One of the world's largest dragonflies is the Giant Petaltail. It is at least six inches (15 cm) from wingtip to wingtip.

Do dragonflies ever hurt people?

No. Even if a dragonfly did bite, a person would barely feel it.

How long have dragonflies existed?

A long time! Scientists have found fossils of dragonflies that lived at the same time as dinosaurs! These remains teach them about dragonflies from long ago.

Important Words

abdomen (AB-duh-muhn) the back part of an insect's body.

hatch to be born from an egg.

marsh an area of low, wet land.

mate to join as a couple in order to reproduce, or have babies.

organ a body part that does a special job. The heart and the lungs are organs.

prey an animal hunted or killed by a predator for food.

protect (pruh-TEHKT) to guard against harm or danger.

shed to cast aside or lose as part of a natural process of life.

thorax the middle part of an insect's body.

Web Sites

To learn more about dragonflies, visit ABDO Publishing Company online. Web sites about dragonflies are featured on our Book Links page. These links are routinely monitored and updated to provide the most current information available.

www.abdopublishing.com

Index

damselflies **4**

defense **16, 26, 27**

dragonfly homes **4, 10, 18**

eating **10, 12, 13, 18, 20, 21, 24,**
    28, 29

egg **8, 9, 10**

eyes **6, 7, 20**

Giant Petaltail **30**

gills **11**

legs **6, 7, 20**

mask **12, 13**

mating **8, 18**

molting **12, 14, 15, 16**

nymph (larva) **8, 9, 10, 11, 12, 13, 14**

predators **16, 24, 25, 26, 27**

wings **6, 7, 12, 16, 17, 22, 23, 26, 30**